Fatherless
NATION

Fatherless NATION

PATRICK ISAAC

FATHERLESS NATION

iUniverse books may be ordered through booksellers or by contacting:

iUniverse
1663 Liberty Drive
Bloomington, IN 47403
www.iuniverse.com
1-800-Authors (1-800-288-4677)

ISBN: 978-1-4917-4042-2 (sc)
ISBN: 978-1-4917-4043-9 (e)

Printed in the United States of America.

iUniverse rev. date: 12/01/2014

Table of Contents

Preface

"Apostle Patrick Isaac has not only inherited the role of spiritual father by vocation, but also the fruits of his ministry demonstrate the revelation of the price and responsibilities attached to it. The impact this book will have on future generations is undeniable."

> Bishop David W. Burton
> *The Resurrection Center*
> *Canada*

"Apostle Isaac is a man of God that we have come to know as a man of wisdom and character and we are honored to call him friend. As a global apostolic leader and father to many, the importance of the spiritual father/spiritual son relationship is critical, and, unfortunately, due to misinformation and a lack of the correct information, many times those relationships do not develop into the totality that they could.

A postle Isaac poignantly speaks to the necessity of that relationship and then lays out a clear and very practical biblical plan to facilitate those relationships God's way. We intend to use this book throughout our organization to enhance what we already teach. 'Fatherless Nation' will do a wonderful job to equip you as a spiritual father or son."

Bishop Dr. Kevin Foreman
Senior Pastor – Harvest Christian Center
Presiding Bishop – Harvest Fellowship of Churches
USA

"We have seen a decline in fathers. This is true both naturally and spiritually. Apostle Patrick Isaac has responded to this need. He has written a book that will challenge the leadership of the Church. This book is based on both the Word of God and experience.

I have known Patrick Isaac and I have seen his passion for truth. You will feel it as you read the pages of this book. I believe this passion can be imparted. You can and will receive a passion to see spiritual fathers restored to the Church. The restoration of fathers will bring the Church into a new level of power and authority. God is teaching us the importance of the Church as a spiritual family, and this book will help reinforce this truth. Where there is no vision the people perish. Allow this book to give you a vision for churches with fathers who have a passion to see sons and daughters come into their calling and destiny."

Apostle John Eckhardt
Presiding Apostle - Impact Network
Senior Pastor - Crusaders Ministry
USA

"Fatherlessness is probably the greatest curse in the history of any nation. It is certainly one of the most destructive social trends in modern history. Spiritual fatherlessness is by far one of the greatest weaknesses and spiritual gaps we are experiencing in our churches and communities today.

The book "Fatherless Nation" by Apostle Patrick Isaac exposes many of the social, psychological and spiritual legacies of fatherlessness in our communities: radical independence, chronic rebellion, pervasive insecurity, identity crisis and spiritual drought. This book gives a deliberate and powerful response to an incredible need in the global church. The book "Fatherless Nation" calls the Church to reclaim God's standard for educating and preparing next-generation Church leaders and ministries. As an apostle of a global network with a global vision to bring global change, I highly recommend this book to create awareness, provide some solutions, and bring some clarity to an ongoing need in the Body of Christ. Spiritual fathering in our generation has the capacity and scope to correct the outstanding dysfunction that exists in our global communities and societies."

Apostle Eliseus Joseph
Apostolic Teaching Centre
Barbados

Introduction

As we take a glimpse at today's society, we can undoubtedly notice the social issues that we are facing. The rate of single parenthood is on the rise. The divorce rate is on the rise. Cohabitation has become the norm in various regions. The homosexuality phenomenon has become more and more prevalent in certain nations. It is very common to see children born out of wedlock with different parents. That is, three brothers and sisters can be related by blood with their mom, yet each can have a different father. Social professionals have enormous difficulty managing problems that society is encountering with the youth. In many countries, the street gang phenomenon has reached epidemic proportions. Drug use has penetrated schools and affected students at an appalling level. Youths are having their first sexual encounters at ages still shy of puberty. Juvenile pornography and juvenile and young adult prostitution are overwhelming police force strategists. Yet, we cannot be surprised at this catastrophic decay of the family core because we cannot remove God and His Word from a society without experiencing disastrous repercussions. The Creator has established the principles necessary for the success and fulfillment of His Creation. The refusal to recognize and to practice these principles can only hinder and negatively affect society. Whether we like it or not, our society needs Jesus.

You see, the common denominator for a society is the family unit. Whether we look at a community, a society, or a nation, the family unit is their common denominator. Thus the sources of social dysfunction in a nation will most definitely be found in its families. When the families of a nation are dysfunctional, there will be a direct impact on the efficiency of that nation. The strength of a nation is therefore connected to the strength of the families in a nation. The devil is strategic – he knows that if he can destabilize the family core by bombarding it with all kinds of plagues, he will be able to affect the nation whose very foundation is comprised of families. The devil knows that there is only one God and he trembles (James 2:19). He knows that the principles of God are immutable and the refusal to put these principles into practice will be catastrophic for man and simultaneously advance *his* kingdom. Thus, for each nation in particular, after having observed their culture, manners and livelihood, he sends appropriate attacks to affect the families of that society in order to have the greatest impact.

The Word of God tells us in this portion of the Scripture,

GENESIS 1:27-28

"So God created man in his own image, in the image of God
He created him...Then God blessed them, and God said to
them, Be fruitful and multiply; fill the earth and subdue it:
have dominion over the fish of the sea, over the birds of the
air, and over every living thing that moves on the earth."

In this verse depicting the creation of mankind, we see God commanding mankind to procreate, subdue the earth and maximize the profitability of its richness. He also commanded them to have dominion over all living things. It is important to notice that both the man and the woman received that order from God. However, He clearly gave the man spiritual authority over humanity and over his family.

GENESIS 2:16-17

"And the Lord God commanded the man, saying, 'Of every tree of the garden you may freely eat; but of the tree of the knowledge of good and evil you shall not eat, for in the day that you eat of it you shall surely die."

As much as it is clear that God speaks to both the man and the woman in *Genesis 1:27-28*, it is also equally clear that He is speaking specifically to the man in the previous verses by using "you", the singular pronoun, to depict the direct order given to the man. The Bible continues with the same concept in the New Testament where the Lord Jesus speaking to the man in Ephesians 5:23 said,

"For the husband is head of the wife, as also Christ is head of the church; and He is the Saviour of the body."

Notice in this verse the authority that God confers to man over his wife and hence over his family. The spiritual authority given by God to man is emphasized in the book of Genesis when, after the original sin of mankind, the Lord God first addresses the one to whom authority was conferred.

GENESIS 3:9-12
"Then the Lord God called to Adam and said to him, 'Where are you?' So he said ... And He (Lord God) said... Then the man said..."

You see, in order for sin to enter into mankind, the devil had to bring the man to sin. The Bible tells us after the beguiling of the serpent:

GENESIS 3:6-7
"So when the woman saw that the tree was good for food, that it was pleasant to the eyes, and a tree desirable to make one wise, she took of its fruit and ate. She also gave to her husband with her, and he ate. Then the eyes of both of them were opened, and they knew that they were naked..."

Notice that the eyes of both the man and woman opened only when the man ate from the fruit that his wife had already eaten. Sin was consummated when the man who was in authority disobeyed the commandment that the Lord God had given to him. Since he was the spiritual authority established by God, sin could not have fully entered mankind if man had not subjected himself. The devil, understanding authority, knew he had to make man succumb in order for sin to fully enter mankind. This truth still remains – in order to notably affect society, the devil absolutely needs to hit directly or indirectly the family unit. In order to do this he needs to affect man since he is the spiritual head of the household.

We see the repercussions of this biblical truth when we witness the impact that a dysfunctional husband has within his family. He drastically increases the probability of the household being destroyed. It clearly is easier for a family to be set in order and restored when the husband is fully functional than when the pious, functional woman tries to set a dysfunctional husband on his proper path for this purpose. This striking truth also stands in the spiritual restoration of a household. It is easier for a husband who receives Jesus Christ as Lord of his life to lead his family in the path of salvation than a woman who receives the Lord and tries to lead her husband away from the path of perdition. Let it be known that the devil is blatantly behind the destruction of men. Even when a man receives Jesus as his Lord and Saviour he struggles to become spiritually sound. Often he will have much more difficulty in growing spiritually than the woman. Where a woman will passionately participate in the work of the Lord, praise and worship wholeheartedly, seek to diligently obey the voice of the Lord and observe carefully His commandments, we see an uncanny battle for many men to do the same. Why? Because the enemy of our souls knows that if the man is in proper position – whether in the secular world or in the Body of Christ – the probability of his household being in place and able to prosper increases exponentially. The enemy aware of this fact, strategically affects the family unit by striking the man of the house. Thus many people grow up with a dysfunctional father or the absence of a father's influence in the household. Multitudes of men and women in many nations are fatherless.

They are affected from the lack of a positive fatherly influence in their lives. Unfortunately, many are suffering relationally, socially and even professionally from this lack without even knowing it. The advancement of the Kingdom of God upon the earth is bringing salvation to a multitude of people from all nations. However, the Body of Christ is facing a major situation – answering to the need of a *father* for the newborn in Christ, and for Christians that did not have one in their lives. We are faced with a fatherless nation. We are facing a generation that had no or very little positive influence from their fathers. We have a generation screaming: "I want to know my father! I want to experience the positive influence and the blessing of a father! I want to experience the love and security of a father!" A fatherless nation is entering the Kingdom of God and is seeking to worship "God the Father" – a Father whom they have had no physical example of. This situation cannot be overlooked since many are in the Body of Christ but are struggling in their growth due to the lacking presence of a natural father. I speak of natural fathers and not biological fathers because a man may be a biological father without ever fulfilling the role of a father in his child's life. Therefore, the natural father designates the one who takes the role of father for a child in his life whether he is the biological father or not. When we look at today's households and how they function, we have kids growing without the presence of their biological father, or with a stepfather, or with someone who is simply the mother's partner and is fulfilling a father's role to the best of his ability. So, I therefore speak of natural fathers, biological or not, who fulfill the role of father in a child's life. Many saints have not had a natural father, but they need a spiritual father.

They have a brother and sister who help them in the Lord, but no spiritual father. They have ministry teams that help them in their growth, but not a spiritual father. They have a pastor who can give them good teaching, but not a spiritual father. When we look at the situation in the Body of Christ we can see the lack of understanding and revelation regarding spiritual fathers. The Lord has given me a burden concerning the need for revelation in this specific area in the Body of Christ. Therefore, knowing that there are different ways that this subject may be addressed, I would like to share with you certain revelations that the Lord has given me on spiritual fatherhood. I believe that the Holy Spirit will enlighten and help the Body of Christ understand and fully benefit from this spiritual principle. It is clearly biblical and is ever so important in this generation and time.

1

Biblical Authenticity of the Revelation of the Spiritual Father

To be able to fully grasp the biblical authenticity of the revelation of the spiritual father, we will have to step out of the religious mentality of a church with a pastor who is the so-called "saviour" of that church. We must go deeper in our revelation of the Word of God to leave our superficial and restrained vision of the church and enter into the revelation of the Body of Christ and of the Kingdom of God. Our God sent His Son on this earth not simply to die for our sins and give us eternal life, but to establish His Kingdom on the earth and see it advance to the extremities of the earth. In order to fulfill this mandate, spiritual fathers will be needed to edify the subjects of the Kingdom so that they might fully apprehend it.

The spiritual truth of spiritual fatherhood is a principle that is seen as much in the Old as in the New Testament. As such, it is a principle that is well established in the Kingdom of God. As we focalize our spiritual understanding on the story of Elijah and Elisha we are able to see this principle in the Old Testament.

After Elijah fled from Jezebel, the witch, he spent some time in the desert. Here the Lord tells him in 1 Kings 19:15-16,

> "... Go, return on your way to the wilderness of Damascus; and when you arrive... you shall anoint... Elisha the son of Shaphat of Abelmeholah... as prophet in your place."

Then in 1 Kings 19:19-21,

> "So he departed thence, and found Elisha the son of Shaphat who was ploughing... and Elijah passed by him, and cast his mantle upon him. And he left the oxen, and ran after Elijah, and said, 'Let me, I pray thee, kiss my father and my mother, and then I will follow thee.' And he said unto him, 'Go back again: for what have I done to thee?' ... then he arose, and went after Elijah, and ministered unto him."

Elijah, the Prophet, obeyed the order that he had received from the Lord to take young Elisha under his wing in order to train him to be his replacement in the prophetic office. We read that young Elisha left his natural father and mother and followed Elijah. Elisha was not an orphan; he lived in the company of both his biological parents, and they had love for their son. That fact was confirmed by Elisha's heart's desire to spend some time with them to show them respect before leaving with Elijah the prophet.

At the end of Elijah's ministry and the beginning of Elisha's mandate as a fully grown prophet, the role of the spiritual father that Prophet Elijah played in young Elisha's life was to be confirmed.

2 KINGS 2:1

"...When the LORD was about to take up Elijah into heaven by a whirlwind, that Elijah went with Elisha from Gilgal."

2 KINGS 2:9-13

"...When they had crossed over, that Elijah said to Elisha, "Ask! What may I do for you, before I am taken away from you?" Elisha said, "Please let a double portion of your spirit be upon me."... as they continued on and talked, that suddenly a chariot of fire appeared with horses of fire, and separated the two of them; and Elijah went up by a whirlwind into heaven. And Elisha saw it, and he cried out, "My father, my father, the chariot of Israel and its horsemen!" So he saw him no more. And he took hold of his own clothes and tore them into two pieces. He also took up the mantle of Elijah that had fallen from him..."

The day that the Lord God decided to take away Elijah the Prophet from the earth, he had departed from Gilgal accompanied by his servant Elisha. Elisha had refused adamantly to leave his master Elijah. After having crossed the Jordan together, Elijah, sensing that his hour had come to depart, asked Elisha what he wanted as a blessing from him. Elisha, stunningly and boldly, asked for a double portion of his spirit, making reference to the portion that normally belongs to the legitimate first son in the Jewish culture (see *Deuteronomy 21:17*). Elisha recognized Prophet Elijah as a father. Having a biological father, it is clear that Prophet Elijah was fulfilling the role of a spiritual father in the life of Elisha. He was the one chosen by God to train him and guide him into his divine destiny. In this spiritual position that Elijah had in Elisha's life, the traits of a natural father were manifested for spiritual growth and maturity necessary for Elisha's ascension into the prophetic office that God had reserved for him. This relationship between Elijah and Elisha was not simply one of a trainer and his trainee, but that of a father and a son. The love of a father for his son is demonstrated by the desire of Elijah to bless his son before he transitioned to the Lord. The cry of Elisha, when he saw that Elijah was taken from him, was not: "*Master, Master* or *Prophet, Prophet*", but what was natural for him at the moment of Prophet Elijah's abrupt departure was to affectionately cry out: "*My father, my father!*"

In the New Testament, we see the revelation of spiritual father exemplified in the relationship of the Apostle Paul with his servants, especially with Timothy, Titus and Onesimus.

Four times in the Epistle to Timothy, the Apostle Paul calls Timothy his son and this even though historically and biblically Timothy was not the biological son of the Apostle Paul.

1 TIMOTHY 1:2

"*To Timothy, my legitimate son in the faith...*"

2 TIMOTHY 1:2

"*To Timothy, my beloved son...*"

2 TIMOTHY 2:1

"*Therefore, my son, be strengthened in the grace that is in Christ Jesus.*"

ACTS 16:1-2

"Then came he to Derbe and Lystra and, behold, a certain disciple was there, named Timothy, the son of a certain woman which was a Jewess, and believed, but his father was a Greek: Which was well reported of by the brethren that were at Lystra and Iconium."

From these New Testament texts, we can clearly see the father and son relationship that existed between the Apostle Paul and Timothy. The Apostle manifests his affection for Timothy, who was not his biological but spiritual son. Timothy had a Jewish mother and a Greek father. Regardless, the Apostle Paul considered him his spiritual son and used the possessive pronoun to affectionately address Timothy as *"...My dear beloved son"*. He becomes even more intimate when he, speaking of Timothy, stated that he was his legitimate son in the faith. Thus he made clear the fact that he had an uncontested unique role of spiritual father in the development of Timothy for the work of the ministry. Timothy was most probably converted during the first visit of Paul to Lystra. In his second visit, the man of God takes Timothy with him to be part of his apostolic team. This was done with the recommendation of the brethren in Lystra and Iconium who gave a good testimony of Timothy. It was in that fashion that young Timothy began to grow spiritually under the wings of the Apostle Paul.

Paul also called Titus and Onesimus, sons in the faith:

TITUS 1:4

"To Titus, my son in the faith."

PHILEMON 1:10

*"I pray thee for my son Onesimus, whom I have begotten
while I was in chains."*

The apostolic training of young Titus was so prolific that he
was sent on apostolic missions by the Apostle Paul to put order
and establish elders in Crete. Whereas in the case of his son in the
faith, Onesimus, Paul attests his good conduct and his renewed
character to his old master Philemon, an honourable citizen of
Colossus.

The principle of spiritual fatherhood, however, should not be
boxed up only in a relationship between two people – a father
and son who are always together, like in the instance of Paul and
Timothy. Timothy had a very close bond with the man of God. He
was part of his apostolic team and travelled extensively with the
Apostle Paul for long periods of time. During this time Timothy
was in the intimate entourage of the apostle. Apostle Paul gives
us more enlightenment concerning spiritual fatherhood when, in
an exhortation given to the church of Corinth, he says:

1 CORINTHIANS 4:15-16

*"For though ye have ten thousand instructors in Christ,
yet have ye not many fathers: for in Christ Jesus I have
begotten you through the gospel. Wherefore I beseech you,
be ye followers of me."*

In this portion of the Word of God, Apostle Paul exhorts the
church of Corinth, which he had established some time before.
The church of Corinth was the local church of the city of Corinth.

Since this was the beginning of the church era, there was only one local church in every city. He told them that they could have ten thousand masters in Christ, but they could not have many fathers, for he had begotten them in Christ Jesus. In other words, it is possible for a local church to have many different ministers who are used by God to bless the assembly spiritually; however, it may only have one father. This statement by Apostle Paul opens our understanding in the "fathering" capacity of the apostolic office in the Church. I will elaborate more on this idea in the upcoming chapters. I will for the moment however emphasize the fact that, as seen through this letter of the Apostle Paul to the church of Corinth, he not only had a father-son relationship with Timothy who was in his entourage, but he also had a relationship with many sons that constituted a local church; The Church of Corinth. Although these spiritual sons did not have the constant physical proximity to Paul that Timothy had in travelling with him on the different apostolic trips, this in no way disqualified them from being legitimate sons to Apostle Paul. This is an important revelation because a son who suffers from spiritual ignorance and emotional instability could believe that he must always be with a man of God and maybe even live with him in order to be a spiritual son to him. I once had a baby in the faith who told me that he felt that I was not available enough to him as a father because he did not have what he felt was adequate proximity. He justified that by saying that a biological father is there for his son; therefore if I were truly a father, I would have to also be physically accessible to him. I answered that he was right on one point; I am a father, but a spiritual one, not a biological one. I am in no obligation to bring him to my home after a service, to have breakfast with him, or supper, or to put him to bed at night in order to fulfill the mandate that I have over his life as a spiritual father. I told him that I was fulfilling my mandate as a spiritual father by being there for him and establishing elders capable of giving him the proper covering, care and spiritual nourishment in order to accomplish his destiny in Christ Jesus. You see, I had seen the mistake that this baby in the faith was making concerning his understanding of spiritual fatherhood. We must realize that biblical analogies conveying spiritual principles to natural facts cannot always be taken literally.

As I meditated more on 1 Corinthians 4:15, the Lord has also opened my spirit to another revelational truth. Notice that Apostle Paul told the saints of Corinth that they could not have many fathers. He was even more specific in finishing the phrase by saying that he was the one who begot them, which was literally saying that he was their spiritual father in the faith. This fact is revelational and very relevant in our generation, since, due to ignorance, some Christians believe that they may have many spiritual fathers. I have heard many such discourses by saints and even from different ministry gifts. Through ignorance, they believe that it is possible to have many spiritual fathers, but not according to Apostle Paul. He told the saints of Corinth that they had but one father and many masters. We cannot have one spiritual father in the country that we live in and another in another nation. In the same vein, we cannot have one spiritual father for the apostolic revelation, another spiritual father for faith and another spiritual father for spiritual warfare. When we look at the analogy with the biological father, we should ask ourselves, "Is it possible for a son to have two biological fathers, to be begotten by one mom and three dads?" In the same way that it is unrealistic to think this way, so is it to believe that we may have more than one spiritual father. Now, things get complicated in the fact that we may be in a church for many years and be under the authority of a pastor who is not our spiritual father. The fact that you receive the Lord in a certain church does not necessarily make that church your local church and the pastor your spiritual father. I hear men of God claim their fatherhood over saints, over ascension gifts of Christ upon which they had no proof or credit to make such a claim. The fact that a minister is part of an association or a network does not necessarily make the leader of such a network the spiritual father over all under him. The fact that a man of God ordains another ministry gift according to *Ephesians 4:11* does not automatically give him the position of spiritual father over the ordained minister. The spiritual father position, or the declaration: *"x or y is a son"*, are so often taken too lightly in the Body of Christ. I believe this is due to ignorance, lack of understanding of the role and revelation of the spiritual father. It is also a lack in understanding the depth of the verb *"begetting"* used in *1 Corinthians 4:15* and, in some other cases, pride. How easy it is to claim our fatherhood over someone that we have not taken care of!

Let us take the time to study in depth the revelation of *"begetting"* in *1 Corinthians 4:15* so that we may fully grasp the importance of the role spiritual fathers have and their responsibility that is so important to the advancement of the Kingdom of God on Earth. Men and women are looking for their fathers, but God has an answer for the fatherless nation. He has established leaders in His Church who are able, in the maturity of their call, to walk in the shoes and carry the responsibility of spiritual fatherhood.

2

The Importance of the Role of the Spiritual Father

Knowing the prevailing absence of natural fathers in many households in our society, we cannot underestimate the importance of the presence of spiritual fathers and the fulfillment of their roles in the lives of their spiritual sons in entering the Kingdom of God. Without despising the role of a natural father in one's life, the responsibility of the spiritual father nevertheless transcends that of the natural father.

At the age of twelve, Jesus went up to Jerusalem with his parents, following the Jewish custom of celebrating Passover. Jesus spoke these words in Luke 2:49 when his parents believed that they had lost him, "...Why were you looking for me? Didn't you know that I must be about my Father's business?" Although Jesus' parents had the capacity to inculcate in him the Jewish values of their time, they were unable to give him the necessary equipment that would have enabled him to take care of His Father's business. In fact, they had not yet understood the dimension of the call of God that was upon their son. The Angel Gabriel had prophesied the birth of

Jesus and his earthly mandate to his mother Mary; however, even she had at one time publicly tried to oppose her son's ministry.

The Bible tells us in Mark 3:21, 31-35,

> *"Jesus' parents, knowing what was going on, came to seize him, because they said: 'He has gone mad'... His mother and brothers came, and standing outside called for him. The crowd that was around him said: 'Behold, your mother and your brothers are outside and they are asking for you.' And He answered and said: 'Who is my mother, and who are my brothers? ... For whoever does the will of God, he is my brother, my sister, and my mother.'"*

MATTHEW 10:36
"A man will have as an enemy those of his own household."

While the Lord was in the center of the plan of God for His life, preaching and demonstrating the power of the Gospel of the Kingdom, his mother and brothers had come to bring him back to reason. They thought he had gone mad due to His mindboggling spiritual declarations and the way He was stirring up the religious system and its leaders. Those from His own household, his parents, regardless of the love they had for him, were unable to understand Him, guide Him or equip Him for His divine mandate.

Natural parents have the capacity to bring up their children according to the wisdom they have, and in the way they believe is best. If they are believers, they have the calling to raise their children in the ways of God, so that when they grow older they will not depart from it. However, this personal education must be coupled with the spiritual education and training from the spiritual father in order to help the child fulfill his spiritual destiny. How many children received an excellent upbringing, but still failed to fulfill the divine call of God on their lives? Why is this? It is due to the absence of spiritual supervision from a spiritual father who could have trained and led them into their divine destiny.

The Bible tells us in Ephesians 2:10,

"For we are His workmanship, having been created in Christ Jesus for good works, which God had prepared in advance that we might practice them."

God has a divine plan for every individual who sees the light of day on this earth. However, it is important to understand that it is in the spirit that we are able to discern the things of the spirit, since God is Spirit. We cannot seize the things that pertain to us coming from a God who is Spirit if we lack spiritual understanding. The spiritual father is able both to train us and guide us in the things of the Spirit. There are good works that God has prepared in advance for us to fulfill. However, the beginning of this leading of the Spirit begins at the time of the new birth. You see, every human being is a creature of God made in the image of God. However, the fall of man due to sin has reduced man to a depraved state. Hence, the ways of his own soulish volition at times identify him more in an animalistic state than as a human being created to be a son. Regardless of how harsh this word may seem, when we look at the way men live and some of the actions they do – some being so inhumane and with seemingly no conscience it all looks more like the work of the devil than anything else. By receiving Jesus Christ as Lord and Saviour in our lives and making the Word of God the basis for our lives, we go from being creatures of God to children of God to sons of God.

John 1:12 tells us,

> *"But to all those who received Him, and to those who believed on His name, He gave the power to become children of God..."*

This is how God's work in our lives begins. God begins His masterpiece, which requires us to submit our will to His in order for Him to perfect us, and gives us the capacity to fulfill His call on our lives. Our new birth is therefore the beginning of our wonderful walk led by God, under the covering and ministry of a spiritual father, where we will be able to fulfill the good works that God has prepared for us in advance that we might practice them. Therefore, regardless of the blessings of a rich relationship with our natural father, the presence and ministry of the spiritual father will allow the child of God to maximize his potential and fulfill the good works prepared in advance by God. The training and direction of the spiritual father will facilitate the path that every son singularly has in fulfilling the good works that God prepared for his destiny.

The spiritual father's presence and ministry is so rich that it is even able to cover the absence or inefficiency of the natural father and meet the need of the son. This is why many people growing up in underprivileged sectors, not having the support of a natural father suffer psychological, emotional, and relational problems. The spiritual father is meant to be a remedy in such situations and to stabilize these children of God throughout their spiritual walk. Therefore, a child of God, who is in the right spiritual house appointed by God for him, is able to receive the security which comes from a father-son or father-daughter relationship. This in turn gives the necessary guidance for the fulfilling of the person's destiny. It is so important to have the relationship that comes from the father. Where the natural father failed, the spiritual father is able to take over. Where the natural father has succeeded, the spiritual father takes the baton and continues on course with his spiritual son, bringing him toward his divine destination where his natural father could not carry him regardless of his genuine and great efforts. Therefore, in the best of scenarios, the spiritual father is not there to despise or diminish the work of the natural father, nor seek to take his place, but he stretches out his hand and, through his grace and his gift from God, he unites his efforts with those of the natural father to perfect and help the child of God attain his divine destiny.

3

The "Fatherless" Syndrome

As I took time to observe with my spiritual eyes the situation of the children of God in the Body of Christ, in the local churches, the Lord allowed me to see some revealing facts concerning the child of God that has suffered from paternal absence. By analyzing these signs, you will be able to see the symptoms that affect people who have suffered from the absence of a natural father. You may even be surprised to see through the light brought by these signs that you may have had a lack in regards to a father-son relationship.

Know that God's desire is that every newborn in the faith be part of a local church that has a theocratic and not a democratic structure – a church with a spiritual authority that is able to carry the responsibility of a spiritual father. This local church would be the spiritual family of this believer, allowing him to grow and attain his spiritual destiny through the covering, security, training and direction of the spiritual father of that local church. One who experienced a broken relationship with his natural father will now enter into a new spiritual family. However, he comes with a gap in understanding how to relate to authority. Hence, he is unable or has difficulty relating with the spiritual authority that the spiritual father is called to have over him in the local church. Regardless of his new birth in Jesus Christ, the newborn Christian will have aftershocks of the dysfunctional father-son relationship that he experienced in his past.

A syndrome is defined as, *the pattern of symptoms that characterize or indicate a particular social condition of a group.* I would like to call the different signs exhibited by a child that has experienced deficiencies in the father-son relationship, "*The Fatherless Syndrome*". Now the plausible question to ask is: What are the signs of the "Fatherless Syndrome"?

Independence

By observing the way certain saints function in the local church, we may notice some that have an independence that is somewhat exaggerated or abnormal in regards to the relationship that they have in their spiritual family with their spiritual father. These saints, affected by bruised relationships in their past, will want to function in the Body of Christ while maintaining a minimum link to it. They are in the Body without being attached to the Body. They are in the local family without really wanting the spiritual bond with their spiritual father. They may want to participate in the vision of the local church, but they always remain detached from all official links with the spiritual father. In fact, even the notion of a spiritual family is a problem. Not in the sense that they don't want one, but rather that they have lots of difficulty identifying with one. They will say: "I am serving God in the Body of Christ, and it is God Who counts and not a relationship with human beings who are weak and able to hurt me. I do not need a relationship with a man on the earth who is imperfect and capable of making a mistake. I have an intimate relationship with God; why would I want a father-son relationship that can hurt me?" They will say: "It is God and I. I have my relationship with my God. I have my intimacy with my God." They will take what they need from the teachings and preaching, but more as a participant who is in a class than one who has any real connection to the trainer or teacher. However, God never spoke of receiving training in some centre or other; He spoke of the Body of Christ joined and knit together by what every joint supplies under apostolic leadership in a local house called church (Ephesians 4:16, 1 Corinthians 12:28). Being disconnected and independent from their spiritual father, they receive no guidance or counsel as to the decisions that they take regardless of the impact such decisions may have on their spirituality or on their lives. They refuse support, counsel, and spiritual covering from their spiritual authority. They say: "That's none of his business." They forget the responsibility that God has given the spiritual authority for the spiritual growth of the saints under his charge.

The Bible tells us in Hebrews 13:17,

> *"Obey those who rule over you, and be submissive, for they watch out for your souls, as those who must give account. Let them do so with joy and not with grief, for that would be unprofitable for you."*

Spiritual fathers, as well as the entire eldership that is under them, are responsible for the maturing of the saints that God has given them responsibility over. The spiritual father has a mandate before God to see to it that his spiritual children reach their destiny. Independence, which is so prevalent in one who suffers from the "Fatherless Syndrome", will certainly affect the success of this saint and the mandate that the Lord gave the spiritual father for his spiritual son.

There is therefore a certain type of independence that some saints exhibit that is directly related to a root problem in their past father-son relationship. They will say,

> *"I am in the church, but do not try to get too close to me, to my private life. It is not that I do not need it, but I'm used to functioning alone. In my past, I did not have counsel, encouragement or correction from a father; why should I have them now? I have become used to messing up and picking myself up little by little. Why would I now, in the Lord, need the support of a spiritual father? Give me the principles and let me take care of the rest with my God. I love the church, I love the ministry, I respect you very much Man of God, Woman of God and I so appreciate the ministry which you consistently bring but... let us keep a safe distance, a long distance relationship that keeps you at bay from all that is personal and intimate to me. I see brothers and sisters in the faith who have a wonderful relationship with their spiritual fathers; I too want this but this desire remains carefully sealed in the depths of my heart. I rather be indifferent toward this type of relationship, but I am*

happy for the others. For me, however, it is different. I go to the point of even believing that this is the plan of God for my particular situation. I believe that my unorthodox relationship with my so-called spiritual father is divine; this spiritual illusion is the resultant effect of all the relational sufferings I have gone through with my natural father in the past."

The independence of a saint can be the result of different situations or reasons. However, one of the reasons for carnal independence from spiritual fathers is a poor father-child relationship in the past.

The Insubmission Problem

One of the spiritual cousins of independence in the "Fatherless Syndrome" is insubmission. The saint with the *Syndrome* will oftentimes suffer with a problem of insubmission with regards to his spiritual authority. This insubmission will usually look to him as simply obeying the voice of Almighty God, since he seems to have a privileged relationship with God and needs no one else to communicate God's Word to him. This carnal way of understanding things, which is readily supported by the devil, puts the individual in a position where insubmission is easy to come by. Now imagine additionally that the saint is naturally prideful- what an easy prey for rebellion. Consequently, the devil easily capitalizes on the situation, and inflicts the saint with a curse, the result of insubmission and rebellion. Ultimately the believer finds himself in a serious predicament, which often is nothing but the result of a bad relationship with the natural father. The Word of God tells us in *Hosea 4:6, "My people perish for lack of knowledge..."* Whether or not insubmission and rebellion stemmed from past hurts, ignorance and disobedience to the principles of gratefulness and submission to established authorities, they will inevitably attract a curse.

Romans 13:1-2 tell us,

> *"Let every soul be subject to the governing authorities. For there is no authority except from God, and the authorities that exist are appointed by God. Therefore whoever resists the authority resists the ordinance of God, and those who resist will bring judgement on themselves."*

This is why, regardless of past hurts, the saint who manifests insubmission will attract condemnation to himself. Unfortunately, he may justify his insubmissive behaviour toward his spiritual father by blaming it on the past in regards to his relationship with his natural father. Some perish by lack of knowledge, and others perish by the disobedience they exhibit in light of the knowledge they have. In one's life, it is certainly an injustice to have such an important person as the natural father not properly fulfill his role. Nonetheless, the repercussions of such a situation, if not treated, will affect a person even after his conversion. They can affect the biblical walk he has in his spiritual family. In the same way, insubmission may be the resultant repercussions of a problematic paternal relationship.

Now, rebellion is linked with insubmission, since the saint who suffers from this disposition can very well know the principles of respect and submission, and still display insubmission which would make the latter rebellion in the Lord's eyes. We can see this type of manifestation when the spiritual leader makes a decision that this saint is not in total agreement with. This saint, being under the influence of rebellion, will see the decision making process of the spiritual father as resembling the decision making process of his natural father who had hurt him before. The result of such an erroneous assessment would invariably be rebellion against the decision taken by his spiritual father. The spiritual authority says left, but the wounded goes right. The spiritual son says: "Let's go forward", the rebellious says, "I do not feel like it" or "I'm not a machine. God did not give me the go-ahead." Every normal reaction of a son toward his father's decisions might be questionable or abnormal to a believer who is biased due to a conflict-filled past relationship. Please understand that this type of carnal reaction is an example of independence and disobedience. The latter duo are not acceptable to God but are directly linked to insubmission and rebellion.

The enemy knows how to affect the sight of the hurting saint, and lead him to do things that are unacceptable and contrary to the Word of God. Therefore, the decisions and actions taken by the spiritual authority are seen through fogged and biased glasses and give an altered reality due to the hurts and pains of a perturbed natural father-son relationship. This, however, in no way changes the fact that insubmission and rebellion will not be tolerated or fall short of judgement by the Word of God.

Discomfort in the Presence of the Father

Another sign of a child of God who has suffered in his relationship with his natural father is the uneasiness he will exhibit when he is in the presence of his spiritual father. This uneasiness will be so apparent that all those who have spiritual eyes will see it. While it is normal for spiritual children within a spiritual house to be comfortable and be at ease in the presence of their spiritual father, he who lived through different hurts in the past with his natural father will have a totally different experience. He will not be able to hide his discomfort in the presence of his spiritual father. This is not only seen in his inability to express himself with his spiritual leader, but it would even be seen in his posture when he listens to the ministry of the spiritual father. This uneasiness would be visible in the way he approaches the spiritual father as well as in his attitude toward him. On the other hand, there is a stark contrast of comfort for the believer who is experiencing a sound father-son relationship. The suffering child may be excessive in following protocol or have an unnecessary rigidity in his interactions with his spiritual authority. Although he (the hurt son) would like to experience the sharing and fellowship with the spiritual father as the other sons, the past pains of a failed biological father-son relationship seem an insurmountable obstacle. You see, being the spiritual head and spiritual father in our apostolic house, I had to deal with many saints who lived through difficult situations with their own natural fathers. This previous situation made their relationship with me very complicated. I still remember a certain sister who was simply unable to be herself in my presence even when I would approach her. She would be laughing or sharing gregariously with other saints. She would even be comfortable with the other elders in PQL Center, but once I would get close, her countenance would change. I would literally feel her discomfort. Her smile was not genuine, she would laugh even at things that were not funny, and she would not be able to get her words out right. She would even take a distant and disinterested attitude, which was clearly the result of her discomfort. When I inquired of her about this, I discovered that she did not have a good relationship with her father, and that was affecting her relationship with me.

Insecurity

One of the responsibilities of a father in a family is to bring security to his children. This implies both physical and psychological security. This security will enable the child to believe in himself, to blossom in his family relationship relationally and academically. Through the security given by the father, the son is able to positively handle his failures. The child therefore develops the right attitude toward failures. He knows how to draw from them the necessary lessons which make him stronger, instead of being discouraged and depressed because things did not go as planned. Through the security that the natural father brings, he will know how to humbly and wisely take advantage of his victories.

The security that the father brings to his child is therefore priceless. When it is absent for whatever reason, there may be some serious repercussions on the child's life. Regardless of the new birth experience, a child that has suffered from an absent father figure may experience insecurity in the core of his being. Insecurity may possibly be manifested in different areas of that Christian's life. You may see insecurity in the manifestation of his gifts and talents regardless of how much encouragement and support he may receive. Some of these saints may have an excessive need to have the support and acceptance of others for decisions they make or when they are doing the ministry. They'll have more difficulty dealing with a failure, be it academic, ministerial or relational. Discouragement, anxiety, depression, difficulty or inability to pass over a failure can result from this weakness. Their portion seems to be a constant pull to abandon whatever they begin. The tendency to quit persists despite the fact that all can see the fruitfulness, and what is positive in the work they began be it a secular or ministry project. Although those around such a saint clearly see his gifts and talents, he has trouble believing the compliments and encouragement he receives from his comrades. He may say to himself: "They must be seeing things. I wonder if they see the same person I see in the mirror."

Insecurity is often coupled with feelings of inferiority and a lack of self-confidence. It produces unnecessary battles in the mind of the saint as well as unexplainable relational battles. Without any basis, this believer can feel that no one in the church cares and loves him. He may feel the father favours others over him. In fact, this "insecurity" may in turn often lead him to unhealthy comparisons of himself with others. Such a person would say things like: "I feel she is more beautiful than I"; "He succeeds more than I do"; "I think he is more apt at handling that situation than me"; "I do not think I have his talent"; "I will never be able to do what he does." Some will self-destruct with all their negative comments: "Is there anything good that can come out of me?" "I've been told I have *such and such* a gift, but I don't think I will ever be able to do something with that." These are all too often some of the many destructive comments of "the insecure", and they inevitably have determining and devastating effects on the life of that believer. The Lord once told me while I was preparing a teaching on mindsets: "You are what you think." He who thinks mediocre will be mediocre. He who thinks with excellence will be excellent. Henceforth, oftentimes the negative thoughts of "the insecure" will lead him to function under the level of success that he was destined to live in, and make him forfeit his destiny. He may still succeed in many things, but all too often he would be under par to his maximal capacity had he accepted and manifested his full potential. Can you believe that all this insecurity may simply be the result of a natural father making unhealthy comparisons of his child with others, or a father praising one child more than another? The game of comparison is very harmful in building a child's confidence. These unhealthy comparisons are enough to leave detrimental effects in a child's emotional security. The father has the capacity to build up or to destroy a child, simply as a consequence of his God-given authority. Insecurity can clearly be a direct result of the "Fatherless Syndrome". An insecure leader will have an attitude of insecurity toward the personnel under him or toward those that have a level of responsibility and authority that is superior to his. He may feel threatened in his role or position. He may feel intimidated by a saint who has self-confidence, even though that brother or sister is under his authority. He will be more comfortable with those that openly acknowledge his role and position, whereas he may avoid or be more uncomfortable with those that do not acknowledge openly and unconditionally his leadership. This type of leader will be more sensitive to all actions that he considers a direct attack on his person.

Insecurity, in this way, will affect the destiny of a child of God. It literally destabilizes the destiny of the believer. Notice, it is very difficult to fully and liberally follow the path God has destined for us when we suffer from insecurity. Even when we are in the center of the will of God there will still be some opposition. Opposition is part of the equation in the perfect plan of God for our lives.

The Bible tells us in Deuteronomy 28:1-13,

> "Now it shall come to pass, if you diligently obey the voice of the Lord your God, to observe carefully all His commandments... The Lord will establish you over all the nations of the earth. And all these blessings will come upon you, and overtake you... you will be blessed in the city, blessed in the country... blessed when you enter, blessed when you go, The Lord will cause your enemies who rise against you to be defeated before your face; they shall come out against you one way and flee before you seven ways... The Lord will open to you His good treasure, the heavens to give the rain to your land in this season, and to bless all the work of your hand. You shall lend to many nations, but you shall not borrow. And the Lord will make you the head and not the tail; you shall be above only and not be beneath, if you heed the commandments of the Lord your God, which I command you today, and are careful to observe them." (NKJV)

Notice that God did not say in His Word that there would never be opposition in the walk toward the fulfillment of our destiny. However, in being obedient to diligently listen to God's voice, by carefully obeying His commands, by observing the Word of God, and remaining faithful in the way, He guarantees the blessing. He guaranteed the blessing, but not the blessing without opposition. Opposition is part of the equation of our lives. Know that the child of God will have opposition; things will not always be "spick-and-span". On the rose of Christianity there are also some thorns. Opposition will be on the path to your blessing. Insecurity affects our reaction to opposition. "The insecure" has much difficulty overcoming opposition. He will have a tendency to be discouraged and even abandon the plan of God because of the difficulties he encounters. It is therefore an undeniable fact that insecurity is one of the signs of the "Fatherless Syndrome".

4

Man of God,
Where is Your Father?

In this season where the Holy Spirit is putting order in His Body, many ascension gifts of *Ephesians 4:11* are realizing that they need the spiritual covering, as well as the input and support of a spiritual father, in order for them to fulfill their destiny. This search is wholesome for it demonstrates a desire to conform to God's Word. However, it must be done with an understanding in the revelation of spiritual fatherhood.

Unfortunately, many attribute the role of spiritual father to men of God who, although they might have a fine ministry, do not necessarily fulfill the role of the spiritual father for these servants of God. I have already heard a servant of God declare that he had two spiritual fathers, and another declare that he had a spiritual father for every sector of his ministry. Some others periodically change spiritual fathers while others are content in having many. Some enter apostolic networks and believe that their commitment to that network is enough to make the founder or presiding minister their spiritual father. My question in response to these kinds of beliefs is the following: Can a child have two biological fathers? The answer is obvious: No, a child has but one biological father. As things are in the natural, so are they in the spiritual. Henceforth, spiritual or biblical truths are often transmitted to us for our understanding via analogies of natural or temporal truths. It is important to understand that when God makes these analogies it is understood that the natural or temporal truths are correctly functional. Therefore, when we want to make a comparison with the spiritual father and the natural father, it is understood that the natural father fulfills correctly his role of natural father. This is why, in the same way that we cannot have many biological fathers, we cannot have many spiritual ones either. The Apostle Paul by the inspiration of the Holy Spirit explains in 1 Corinthians 4:15,

"For though you have ten thousand masters in Christ, you don't have many fathers, since it is I who have begotten you."

In other words, many servants of God can be used by God to bless you, but you can have only one spiritual father. They can be used by God to bring you enlightenment in a specific area or principle of the Word of God. They can be used to propel you into your next level without being your spiritual father. The spiritual father is neither transferable nor negotiable. There are not two or three. He is not your spiritual father only when it pleases you. You can even go physically very far away from him and be positively influenced by other men of God, but the biblical and spiritual fact still remains that you can only have one spiritual father. It is with that spiritual understanding that Apostle Paul boldly declared to the saints of Corinth that he is their father, he begat them in the Lord; it is not Apollos, it is not Cephas nor any other minister even if they have been or still are a rich blessing to them in the ministry. "...for in Christ I have begotten you through the Gospel" (*1 Corinthians 4:15*, KJV). In essence, "I am your father." It goes without saying how hard this statement can be for the ignorant, immature, carnal or unstable Christian. Such a statement would be viewed as simply another authority of abusive character seeking to control and dominate. Nevertheless, the statement of Apostle Paul made to the people of God at Corinth – that he was their spiritual father – remains biblically accurate.

5

You Told You that
You are a Spiritual Father?

At this juncture for this teaching, it is imperative to point out the characteristics of a spiritual father. The need is obvious in the Body of Christ, and those that are truly mandated by God for this mandate are in the Body of Christ. Nonetheless, in observing evangelical circles, many carry the title of spiritual father; some are self-proclaimed spiritual fathers without possessing the characteristics or administrating the ministry that a spiritual father is called to bring to a spiritual son. Please understand that spiritual fatherhood is much more than a title. What superficiality to see some attribute to themselves the title of spiritual father without clearly fulfilling their functions as a father to their so-called sons in the faith! Because a man of God is used to ordain a servant of God in a ministry does not automatically attribute to him the title of spiritual father. The fact that a minister realizes the advantages and blessings of being in an apostolic network does not automatically make the leader of that network his spiritual father. Just because a man of God was used to bring light through a particular revelation to someone does not make him a spiritual father. I may shock some by saying that a minister may have been in a local church for years yet the senior pastor may not be his spiritual father.

So what are the characteristics and the ministry that authenticate spiritual fatherhood? I believe that you have been holding your breath long enough. Therefore, without further ado, before you call me a heretic and before you get rid of this book, take the time to consider these characteristics and the ministry which the Lord has enlightened me in concerning the subject of spiritual fatherhood.

6

The Spiritual Father
has the Capacity to Beget

EPHESIANS 4:11-12

"And He himself gave some to be apostles, some prophets, some evangelists, some pastors and some teachers, for the equipping of the saints for the work of the ministry, for the edifying of the Body of Christ."

1 CORINTHIANS 12:28

"And God has appointed these in the church: First apostles, second prophets, third teachers..."

1 CORINTHIANS 4:14-16

"I do not write these things to shame you, but as my beloved children I warn you. For though you might have ten thousand instructors in Christ, yet you do not have many fathers; for in Christ Jesus I have begotten you through the gospel. Therefore I urge you, imitate me."

The Lord Jesus Christ has given five gifts to the church for its perfecting and edification. However, when we take a spiritual look at these five ministry gifts, we can see the preeminence of the apostolic office. The apostle is named first in *Ephesians 4:11* and in *1 Corinthians 12:28*. As we study the ministry of the apostle, we discover the great spiritual responsibility and spiritual authority that this office has in the Body of Christ. Many profound men of God have been used insightfully by God to expound revelationally on the ministry of this ascension gift for the edification of the Body of Christ. Among these men is Apostle John Eckhardt, a spiritual general of the 21st Century in the Body of Christ who has written many valuable books on the apostolic ministry. God endows the apostle with a tremendous spiritual capacity to establish churches. One of his many graces is the capacity he received from God to "beget". When reading *1 Corinthians 4:14-16*, we see the Apostle Paul, without pretention, addressing the saints of the church at Corinth as his beloved children saying that he is the father that begat them in Christ. The apostolic office has received the capacity from God to spiritually father the saints of the Kingdom of God in the local church.

You see, in the Corinthian culture, the upper echelon of that society had servants and guardians who would accompany the young sons to school and take care of them. So Apostle Paul uses the cultural reality of that time to tell the saints of Corinth that they may have had many spiritual guardians (such as Apollos) who were taking care of them, and keeping them in the faith. However, they did not have many fathers, for it was he who had begotten them in Jesus Christ. Many learned theologians limit the Apostle Paul's claim of being the Corinthian saints' father only to the extent that he led them to the Lord, and founded the church of Corinth. With all due respect to these scholars, I believe that the capacity to beget in a biblical sense transcends the fact of simply bringing someone to the knowledge of Jesus Christ. Otherwise, any Christian who brings another person to the Lord in a legitimate way would automatically become the spiritual father of that new born in Christ.

What are we to say of Evangelists, who bring multitudes of people to Jesus Christ? Are they for this simple fact the fathers of these multitudes? Absolutely not! The responsibility of spiritual fatherhood transcends that of the new birth, and to put the first stepping-stones in the life of the new believer in the local church. When we meticulously and spiritually analyze the ministry of Apostle Paul to the Corinthians, we will see that this master builder had deposited some solid foundations in that local church that was able to propel the people into their destiny. To beget, in its full biblical revelation, literally means to give birth and deposit the necessary foundations thereby enabling the nurturing and blossoming of the spiritual child or children for the fulfilling of their spiritual destiny. The responsibility is certainly greater than simply bringing someone to the Lord or merely giving some basic faith and fundamental principles. The Apostle Paul spoke of his ministry to the Corinthian people saying,

1 Corinthians 1:4-8
"I thank my God always concerning you for the grace of God which was given you in Christ Jesus, that in everything you were enriched in Him, in all speech and knowledge, even as the testimony concerning Christ was confirmed

---

in you, so that you are not lacking in any gift, awaiting eagerly the revelation of our Lord Jesus Christ, who will also confirm you to the end, blameless in the day of our Lord Jesus Christ."

In eighteen months, the Apostle Paul deposited such a depth of revelation in the saints of the church of Corinth that they had all the riches concerning the word and knowledge, with the testimony of Christ Jesus being solidly established in them. He had done more than simply preaching a few evangelical messages in order to bring them to salvation and accomplishing a few miracles so that the people would recognize the power that resides in the Kingdom of God. The gifts of the Spirit were not uncommon to them; they possessed them all. Apostle Paul had clearly done an in-depth work in the establishment of the church of Corinth. He was rightfully allowed to speak of the people of Corinth as being his children in the faith. He was truly their spiritual father.

In the same way that the husband is placed in authority in a God- fearing household, the apostle is placed in authority in the spiritual home according to *1 Corinthians 12:28*. One of the major reasons for this position of authority is his divine capacity to beget, to give birth to, and to work at the maturing of God's people for the fulfillment of their destiny in Christ Jesus. Apostle Paul declares in 1 Corinthians 9:1-2,

"Are you not my work in the Lord? ... for you are the seal of my apostleship in the Lord..."

What validated his spiritual fatherhood of the people of God at Corinth was not simply the fact that he had given birth to them spiritually, or the fact that he had given them revelation on a certain principle in the Word. It was rather that, through his teachings, he had given them the necessary tools to be solidly anchored in their faith in Jesus Christ and be positioned for the fulfillment of their spiritual destiny. Therefore, the question to you is: Who has been instrumental in giving you not simply some messages, but a solid foundation and the biblical truths which have been or are paramount to the fulfillment of your maturity? Furthermore, who has nurtured you to the realization of who you are in Christ to allow you to reach your destiny in Christ Jesus?

7

The Spiritual Father Helps his Son Discover his Spiritual Identity

The Apostle Paul speaking to his legitimate son in the faith, Timothy, says the following,

1 TIMOTHY 1:18
"This charge I commit to you, son Timothy, according to the prophecies previously made concerning you..."

2 TIMOTHY 1:5-6
"...When I call in remembrance the genuine faith that is in you, which dwelt first in your grandmother Lois and your mother Eunice, and I am persuaded is in you also. Therefore I remind you to stir up the gift of God which is in your through the laying on of my hands."

We see here in these verses Apostle Paul sharing on the spiritual identity of his legitimate son in the faith, Timothy. He recalled to Timothy that his identity was recognized through the prophetic word and the laying on of the hands that he received from him. In the example of Apostle Paul, a spiritual father has the capacity and grace from God to help their spiritual sons discover who they are in the Lord. Unfortunately, many Christians spend years under the covering of a man of God without ever discovering their spiritual identity in Christ Jesus. Whereas, when you get in contact with your legitimate father in the faith who walks you through your ministerial process, he will be able to help you find your spiritual identity. You will not be released in his identity but in yours. He will not impose upon you who he is or even the part of the plan of God for his life that he failed in or that he did not have the courage to fully accomplish, but you will be enlightened in your own spiritual identity. I have witnessed particular congregations where everybody speaks like the pastor, walks like the pastor, dresses in the same style as the pastor. Those that bring the Word to the congregation, preach like the pastor. We would surely think that we are in a soft drink plant manufacturing a single product with a single brand and a single flavour. But such is not the will of God. This is why the apostolic office has been established as first in the Body of Christ. The apostle has the capacity as spiritual father to release originals and not copies in the Church of God. If you were to observe sons of an apostle in their mature state, you would clearly see them with their own spiritual identity. By this fact, the apostolic office is able to release different gifts as well as gifts in the same office, and the gifts in the same office will each have their particularities, with different graces and different mandates. A fathering apostle may have many sons that are called to the prophetic office, but he will be able to identify them in their respective gifts and graces. One may therefore be a governmental prophet, another one a

Shamar prophet powerful in intercession and spiritual warfare, another one a social prophet and another one an administrative prophetess. All are prophets, but are identified in their gifting, graces and respective mandates. The spiritual father helps his sons clarify their horizons. His spiritual children will not have to walk on each other's feet in the ministry. They will not have to overlap the ministry of another, but they will be identified and joyfully and blissfully maximize who they are and what they are called to do in the Lord. There is no need to be jealous or to compete against each other, since all in the Body of Christ have their position and their importance in the fulfillment of the plan of God. The Lord has prepared a good work for us to accomplish. He uses the spiritual father for our spiritual identification in order that we might accomplish the good works that have been prepared by the Lord for us.

8

The Spiritual Father Educates and Trains Spiritually

2 TIMOTHY 1:13
"Hold fast the pattern of sound words which you have heard from me in faith and love which are in Christ Jesus."

The spiritual father does not only have the capacity to spiritually identify his spiritual children, but he is also able to educate and train them spiritually. Apostle Paul told his spiritual son, Timothy, to hold fast the pattern of sound words that he received from him. Timothy had therefore been educated and trained by his spiritual father, Apostle Paul, in the ministry. As much as a natural child needs to be educated and trained by his parents, a child that enters the spiritual family of God needs also to be educated and trained spiritually. This spiritual upbringing may even incorporate the care the spiritual child did not receive from his natural parents. The spiritual education and training that the spiritual father gives to his spiritual children are instrumental to the fulfillment of their destiny. They can therefore not be underestimated and neglected. How many premature ministers do we see in the Body of Christ? How many servants of God do we see with flaws in their gifting, then flaws in their character, or vice-versa, or even flaws in both? Why? There has been an absence of a spiritual father or a premature rupture of the educational and spiritual ministerial training process. Truly, for many the calling and potential were there, but the complete spiritual training was lacking.

The son that is wise will accept being fully educated spiritually and ministerially trained before launching into his destiny. And for this he will need certain traits. The son that wants to fully complete his training will need a lot of humility.

Proverbs 16:18 says,

> *"Pride goes before destruction and a haughty spirit before a fall."*

Chapter 18:12 continues by saying,

> *"Before destruction the heart of a man is haughty, and before honour is humility."*

Then 1 Corinthians 8:2 adds,

> *"And if anyone thinks that he knows anything, he knows nothing yet as he ought to know."*

Understand that a prideful son will have difficulty benefiting fully from the education and training of his spiritual father because the proud has difficulty recognizing his true level. He oftentimes believes he masters what he has not mastered at all. Therefore, he brings confusion and spiritual stagnation, since he who thinks that he knows anything, knows nothing yet as he ought to know and cannot therefore think he can grow. We need to understand that the first step toward progress is to recognize one's ignorance. Since the proud has a biased understanding of his ignorance, it is difficult for him to receive from his spiritual father the education and training necessary for his progress.

To remedy this condition, the son that has wisdom will seek to grow in humility to maximize the education and training he is called to receive from his spiritual father. He will have to be conscious of his vulnerability and weaknesses. The truth of God needs to illuminate our vulnerability, weaknesses, and ignorance before it can permit us to progress. When we recognize these shortcomings, we can then benefit from another fruit of the Word: spiritual progress.

There are several periods in the life of the son who receives education and training from his spiritual father. There are the periods of infancy, adolescence, and spiritual adulthood. In every one of these periods, the need of the son differs. Therefore, there is a different need for a different season. There are periods of newness, of apprenticeship, and of revelation. Each has the need for adjustments, corrections and reproof for its success. The spiritual father has no difficulty bringing the necessary adjustments and corrections for the success of his son's training. The Bible tells us,

PROVERBS 15:10
"Harsh discipline is for him who forsake the way, and he
who hates correction will die,"

"It is better to hear the rebuke of the wise than for a man to hear the song of fools,"

Correction and reproof are part of the ministry that the spiritual father brings. The Lord has given him the grace to encourage and celebrate at the opportune time, as well as to correct and rebuke. A son who wants to dodge correction, who fights correction, who refuses correction, or even runs away from correction, will attract death in the area of his life where the Holy Spirit wants to correct him in his spiritual process. It is undeniable that corrections refused on a son's life, for the shortcomings which the Holy Spirit wanted to take care of will, one day or another, resurface and haunt him in his spiritual walk.

Proverbs 22:15 says,

"Foolishness is bound up in the heart of a child; the rod of correction will drive it far from him."

Whereas Proverbs 23:13-14 declares,

"Do not withhold correction from a child, for if you beat him with a rod, he will not die. You shall beat him with a rod, and deliver his soul from hell."

Here the Bible gives us wisdom in the way to raise up our children. Whether in the case of a natural or a spiritual child, correction should be part of a normal educational process.

Although family psychologists of this 21st century say that one should not physically correct a child, and though governments, ignorant of the wisdom of God in the educational dynamic of children's upbringing, have legislated in agreement with them, the Word of God tells us not to spare the child from the rod. Notice, the Bible does not tell us to physically abuse a child with a rod, but to correct him with a rod when the follies of the child demand it. The Bible is clear that the rod of correction will spare the child from folly. Those who are anti-correction with the rod will say that this particular verse only connects rod with the hardship of correction. However verses 13 and 14 of Proverbs 23 give precision on the subject. The Word clearly states that if we beat a child wisely and opportunely with a rod, he will not die. Rather, the correction with the rod will save his soul from decadence. When a man wants to take his own soulish path and rebel against the Word of God, the consequences always follow, without any doubt. Since certain societies have forbidden parents to physically punish their children, they have also clearly experienced and witnessed escalating negative social issues with their youth. Disrespect, rebellion, insubmission, and kids who want to follow their own whims are only a sample of the social issues that these societies have been encountering. Social professionals have found no rest with the issues of the youth and are only able to diagnose the problems without being able to find any viable and effective prognoses. What is the reason for this? It is disobedience to the Word of God. Their own decisions and legislation have put their feet in their mouth.

Natural parents as well as spiritual parents are called to correct their children. The spiritual father needs therefore to take a stand and correct his spiritual sons, although he needs to do it according to the Spirit and not the flesh. He will not have to correct his spiritual child with a natural rod, but he will have to correct him with the spiritual rod, which is the Word of God. The spiritual father is obliged to sometimes bring correction or to rebuke to his spiritual son which will surely cause some carnal discomfort. Nevertheless, offered with spiritual comfort, it tends toward the saving of his soul. When a spiritual child is divinely corrected by his father, the only part of his being that is negatively affected is his flesh; the spirit can only be edified. Proverbs 15:10 states, *"A harsh discipline is for him who forsakes the way..."* You therefore, who are a son, though you can receive multiple compliments and be constantly encouraged, know that the authentic spiritual father without a doubt will have to correct you or rebuke you sometime. You can neither intercede nor fast for that. It is a normal occurrence in the father-son relationship that is healthy, and favourable to the spiritual child for growth and maturity.

Therefore, spiritual education and training are the portion of a spiritual father that is not only of words but of action. The authentic spiritual fatherhood will not only be used to help you recognize your spiritual identity, but has the necessary capacity to train you through divine revelation. In this way, you will not be a child tossed to and fro. Instead, you will be a servant of God walking in the path of God to manifest the good works that God has prepared in advance for you to accomplish.

9

Releasing Spiritual Blessing

Many adults have grown up with difficulty in recognizing their identity. They grew up without the blessings of a paternal relationship capable of bringing the necessary support to forge in them a strong and positive character, and to permit them to blossom in their destiny and heritage. Therefore, the capacity that a spiritual father has to release spiritual blessings to his spiritual child shines with importance. There are many who receive Jesus Christ and have a dysfunctional family background, as well as others that have been brought up in a single parent home without the presence of a father or father figure. They did not have the opportunity to gain from the father-child relationship. The confidence that a father is able to bring through his encouragement, and his positive decrees over his child, is incomparable.

The Bible tells us in Genesis 27:27-30, 33,

> *"And he came near and kissed him; and he smelled the smell of his clothing, and blessed him and said: 'Surely, the smell*

of my son is like the smell of a field which the Lord has blessed. Therefore may God give you of the dew of heaven, of the fatness of the earth, and plenty of grain and wine. Let peoples serve you, and nations bow down to you. Be master over your brethren, and let your mother's sons bow down to you. Cursed be everyone who curses you, and blessed be those who bless you!' Now it happened, as soon as Isaac had finished blessing Jacob, and Jacob had scarcely gone out from the presence of Isaac his father, that Esau his brother came in from his hunting...Then Isaac trembled exceedingly, and said, 'Who? Where is the one who hunted game and brought it to me? I ate all of it before you came, and I have blessed him and indeed he shall be blessed.'"

We can see in these verses the power of the declaration of a father over a son. After the trickery of Jacob, his father released to him a blessing that was irrevocable, even if the intention of Jacob was to bless his firstborn son Esau. In spite of Esau's distress and his desire to receive the blessing that was the portion of the firstborn, his father had released that blessing upon Jacob and could not take back his word. Therefore, the blessing that Isaac pronounced on Jacob followed him throughout the course of his life. Reading the rest of chapter 27, you will discover that Jacob, by the prophetic decrees of his father, received superiority over Esau and his other brothers, and was their master. His blessings therefore superseded theirs. We can further see, in chapter 49, the prophetic blessings that Jacob declared over his sons and their posterity who became the twelve tribes of Israel. These spiritual blessings were their portion in their entirety.

These two examples are from fathers who recognized their spiritual authority and released the blessings on their children. But we will also see the example of Moses who released spiritual blessings on Joshua who was not his natural son, but his spiritual son. This will permit us to fully grasp the spiritual character of the capacity of a father to release the blessing on his children.

1 Chronicles 23:15 lists the biological sons of Moses,

"The sons of Moses were Gershon and Eliezer."

The Bible also declares in Deuteronomy 34:9,

"Now Joshua the son of Nun was full of the spirit of wisdom, for Moses had laid his hands on him; so the children of Israel heeded him, and did as the Lord had commanded Moses."

Notice Moses had biological sons; however, Joshua distinguished himself as a spiritual son by the quality of his service to Moses. He therefore received the blessing of the mantle of authority that Moses had to lead the people of God. The Lord used him to continue the ministry of Moses. Moses was the liberator used by God to take the people of Israel out of bondage from the hands of the Egyptians, but Joshua was the conqueror used by God to make His people enter the Promised land. Joshua's ministry was initiated by Moses' laying on of hands and releasing spiritual blessings on him. Our verse of predilection says that Joshua was filled with the spirit of wisdom because Moses had laid his hands on him. This spirit of wisdom was in full-fledged operation only after Moses released the blessings on Joshua. As much as the words of Jacob followed his sons, the prophetic words of Moses also accomplished their course. Growing under the teachings and perfecting ministry of a spiritual authority cannot be neglected since it has the capacity to release the spiritual blessings on the spiritual children that God gives.

I would like to elaborate on two particular ways of being anointed for service. There is, first of all, one's work to have a particular and unique anointing without the help of anyone. It is true and biblical that some, by divine election, may develop a particular anointing without having served under a particular ministry that released to them the base of that anointing. This type of anointing can be called patriarchal because it starts a lineage. Jesus had a patriarchal anointing, Abraham had a patriarchal anointing. Apostle Paul also had a patriarchal anointing since he started a ministerial lineage without clearly having a spiritual authority that trained him in the ministry. This situation is quite different from the twelve who were trained by Jesus in his earthly ministry. Jesus had a direct influence on their perfecting for the work of the ministry. The patriarchal anointing starts a lineage and initiates a movement of the Spirit that affects a generation. You should know, however, that this type of anointing is very particular. It is not for "the average Joe" who decides carnally to leave a local house to be directly trained by God without the covering and training of a spiritual father and the elders of the local church. After an analysis and an observation of the workings in the Body of Christ, you will notice that more often than not those who say they have a special call of God and that they are not called to grow under a specific ministry are saints with some character issues. It appears as if they are called to make special pilgrimages to different ministries before launching out in their own ministry. These are the arrogant, full-of-themselves saints under the hold of Leviathan (the demonic principality that infests men with pride). They refuse to submit themselves to anyone in the church where the Lord has placed them to receive adequate training to fulfill their destiny. And this is primarily due to the fact that they cannot accept the necessary corrections for their growth. Instead, they want liberty to do and say what they want, without being accountable to follow the principles of God to grow uprightly.

Nevertheless, there are ministers called by the Lord to a particular process. In these particular cases, the ministers, although they have a spiritual father, receive revelation and specific training from the Lord Jesus Himself. The Lord Jesus Himself imparts to them the necessary truths and principles key to the fulfilling of their divine mandates. Apostle Paul is a good example of such a case. Although the twelve were trained by the Lord, Apostle Paul did not have to go to Jerusalem to be trained by the apostles; rather the Lord Jesus personally trained him, Galatians 1:15-24. This does not mean that they will not grow in a local church and under authority. Yet, there is a genuine and particular anointing that is not fathered by a man of God. It is nurtured through a personal relationship with God, for a certain and specific mandate given by God. The Lord will sometimes appoint in some particular cases, generals of God to participate in the grooming of a patriarchal minister without permitting though that none of these generals rightfully be recognized as the spiritual father. God Himself in His sovereignty chooses and traces the path for such a process. It is imperative to know that this type of process is not decided by the carnal saint struggling with insubmission, pride and biblical ignorance, but God-chosen with patriarchal anointing as a clear fruit of this call in starting a generation, a reform or a movement of the Spirit. The Lord Jesus Christ, Apostle Paul, Moses and Abraham are examples of such patriarchal ministry. They were used to start a generation or a spiritual lineage for Christ. They did not have a spiritual father that overwhelmingly marked their spiritual process. It was through their relationship with God that they were able to give birth to renowned sons. The Lord Jesus raised Apostle Peter, James and John amongst others; Apostle Paul raised Timothy and Titus amongst others; and Moses raised Joshua who is a second-generation apostolic type.

In the majority of cases, the path chosen by God for the transferring of the anointing and the grace for the ministry is through the father-son relationship. Elisha received his spiritual heritage from his spiritual father to start his ministry. After he received the mantle of Elijah that represented the succession of anointing and of prophetic authority, the Bible explains in which fashion Elisha started his ministry.

2 KINGS 2:9-14

"And so it was, when they had crossed over, that Elijah said to Elisha, 'Ask! What may I do for you, before I am taken away from you?' ...And it happened, as they continued on and talked, that suddenly a chariot of fire appeared with

horses of fire, and separated the two of them; and Elijah went up by a whirlwind into heaven... He also took up the mantle of Elijah that had fallen from him, and went back and stood by the bank of the Jordan. Then he took the mantle of Elijah that had fallen from him, and struck the water, and said, 'Where is the Lord God of Elijah?' And when he also had struck the water, it was divided this way and that; and Elisha crossed over."

Elisha started his ministry with the anointing that was on his spiritual father, Elijah, represented by the mantle of the trainer-prophet Elijah. The anointing of God is transferable. One of the representations of the presence of God in the Scriptures is oil. You see, a person that is soaked with oil is able to transfer some of this oil by rubbing-off onto another. Another good example is perfume. A person that gets in contact with one who is perfumed will also smell of the same perfume. Therefore, a saint that serves in a ministry, or a son that rubs on his spiritual father by the teaching and the ministry that his father brings him, will see the grace of his father manifest in his life. I still remember after having interpreted for a man of God for a year and a half, I started ministering with the same type of anointing as this man of God. In fact, after he would finish preaching, he would make an altar call and have two prayer lines; one for him and the other for me. The extraordinary thing is this: The same manifestations of healing, deliverance, and miracles that he had in his line, I saw also in mine. I received an impartation of the anointing on the life of this man of God by simply being submissive and obedient to serve him and receive his teachings. I was able to grow in the ministry of deliverance and healing in that fashion. The mistake that some make though is to start their ministry prematurely. When they see the manifestation of the power of God while they are serving a man of God, they figure this is proof and reason enough to start a ministry. Unfortunately, they omit the importance of growing in maturity and waiting for the timing of God. The anointing that we may manifest while we are serving a man of God or as we are submitting ourselves in the local ministry is functional to start us up in ministry. However, full grown anointing for ministry is received as we grow in the teachings received from our spiritual father and the ministry of the local assembly. We then can reach our full potential in having our own identity in the Lord. In my personal case, although in my first ministerial steps I was ministering like the man of God that I was translating for (to the point that the way I was praying and the tone of my voice resembled his), as I grew in maturity some years later after my pastoral ordination, I had an entirely different way of ministering healing and deliverance. Like Elisha, I started with the anointing that was transferred to me through my service and proximity to the man of God. That anointing then grew to an anointing particular to the call and mandate of God on my life through my spiritual growth in the Lord. It is therefore imperative to understand that it is our duty to wisely receive the impartation that we can receive from our spiritual father to make our first steps in ministry. Do not be prideful and arrogant, wanting to establish a particular anointing and "unique ministry", when you have not received that direction or grace from God.

Elisha did not fall in the trap of individualism, as is common in this era. After witnessing the taking away of his spiritual father in chariots of fire, he recognized that he received the anointing of Elijah. Notice, he declared: "Where is the Lord God of Elijah?" He also struck the water which divided this way and that. Many, ignorant of the revelation of the principle of the spiritual father and of spiritual authority, would have thought Elisha's statement to be heretic, demonic or even idolatrous. These false notions are common since our modern society has so many people who want to be independent, self-trained, self-perfected, and directly led by God without submitting themselves to any spiritual authority. Yet Elisha had grasped the abundant blessing in his relationship with his spiritual father. Furthermore, this first miracle was instrumental, for it brought him the respect of his peers.

The Bible tells us in verse 15,

> "Now when the sons of the prophets who were from Jericho saw him, they said, 'The spirit of Elijah rests on Elisha.' And they came to meet him, and bowed to the ground before him."

The Lord is the One who established the principle of authority, and He will surely put His stamp of approval on it. A spiritual authority has been granted a special grace by God because of his role and responsibility pertaining to the care of the people of God.

The Bible, in Numbers 12:4-9, tell us that after Aaron and Miriam spoke against Moses the servant of the Lord,

"Suddenly the Lord said to Moses, Aaron, and Miriam, 'Come out, you three, to the tabernacle of meeting!' So the three came out. Then the Lord came down in the pillar of cloud and stood in the door of the tabernacle, and called Aaron and Miriam. And they both went forward. Then He said, 'Hear now my words: If there is a prophet among you, I, the Lord, make Myself known to him in a vision; I speak to him in a dream. Not so with My servant Moses; He is faithful in all My house. I speak with him face to face, even plainly, and not in dark sayings; and he sees the form of the Lord. Why then were you not afraid to speak against My servant Moses?' So the anger of the Lord was aroused against them, and he departed."

In this portion of Scripture, the Lord is irate with Aaron and Miriam who dared compare their position and spiritual authority with Moses'. The Lord was very clear in the acute difference that existed between them and His servant Moses. He signified to them that He would communicate through visions which had a certain element of enigma, but He would speak to His servant Moses mouth to mouth. This statement illustrates how directly, and with great clarity, He would speak to the spiritual authority who was over the whole congregation, which included Aaron and Miriam. Aaron and Miriam were delegated authorities under Moses. Moses' authority therefore superseded theirs largely.

It is true that the Lord God loves all His children. Nevertheless, this fact does not change: He grants His visionary, spiritual shepherd or spiritual authority a greater grace to be able to accomplish his mandate by reason of his responsibility and accountability.

Counseling and Support in the Path of our Destiny

One of the tremendous qualities of a mature and seasoned spiritual father is his capacity to support his son in the different seasons of his destiny. You see, the father who loves his spiritual child would love to see him grow in maturity and spirituality. We need to ask ourselves questions then when someone proclaims his spiritual fatherhood and yet either actively or passively does not desire spiritual and ministerial growth for his spiritual children. The mere proclamation of a leader that he is striving to see his spiritual sons blossom, is surely not enough. Concrete actions need to follow his declaration. He should not only talk the walk but also walk the talk. Spiritual growth of the sons needs to follow such a declaration. It is the evident growth and spiritual advancement of the sons' divine destiny that will prove such a declaration. A natural father wants to see his child reach heights that he himself could have only dreamed of. He wants him to go further in his life's success. Similarly, a spiritual father should desire to see his spiritual children reach growth, spiritual heights, and ministerial success that supersede his greatest spiritual and ministerial accomplishments. This fact needs to be understood in the proper context though; i.e. based on the Word, this literally means the Lord wants us to go from glory to glory and faith to faith. The level of faith and glory that a spiritual father has reached should help and nurture his children into greater glory and faith in his children's respective callings and mandates in the Lord. This does not necessarily mean that every spiritual child needs to have a more extensive ministry than his spiritual father. This ambiguity has led many second-generation men of God who had fathers with widely productive ministries and great exposure given by God in the Body of Christ and in the secular world, to a lot of stress. This stress stems from the fact the child felt he had to surpass his spiritual father in deeds or pressure exerted by his peers and society to do more than his spiritual father. We need to remember that although many of the great apostles of the first century church had biological and spiritual children, these children did not necessarily have the level of exposure in the history of the church as their spiritual fathers. Too many second-generation preachers' kids have missed their destiny because of this kind of pressure or the obligation that was impressed on them to be the successor to their father's or mother's impact ministry. They had to constantly live with comparison to their parents' ministry. This is certainly not the will of God, for as children of God we will not be judged in comparison to our spiritual father's ministry, but in the particular calling and mandate that God has given us. A spiritual father will therefore not want to stop the support that he gives his spiritual child in his perfecting until he sees his child reach the spiritual heights that the Lord had destined for him. How tragic to see churches filled with spiritual children that are spiritual cheerleaders to a man or woman with a so called mega-ministry, instead of having spiritual children perfected and equipped by a spiritual father to the fulfillment of their destiny. The authentic spiritual father will see to the blossoming of his spiritual children for the fulfillment of their destiny. He will accept and respect the growth and maturing of his spiritual children.

The spiritual father will recognize the different stages of the spiritual growth of his son. There is infancy, then adolescence, and adulthood. The spiritual authority over this believer needs to recognize these different stages in the spiritual life of the saint because every stage requires a different father-son relationship. A father should not treat a teenager as an infant. There is a level of responsibility and maturity that a teenager should manifest above that of an infant. This disposition is absolutely normal. Imagine a father that follows his child to college because he is overprotective, and thinks that the child cannot handle the precariousness and responsibilities of the collegiate level. That would certainly be exaggerated and absurd. Nonetheless, we see that kind of absurdity at the spiritual level when a spiritual father is not able to recognize the different stages in the spiritual process of his sons, and thus treat them accordingly. The spiritual father cannot permit himself to be overprotective. He needs to know, when the time comes, after proper perfecting and equipping, to let his sons fly with their own wings in the calls and mandates of God on their lives. You see, in each stage in the spiritual process of his son, the spiritual father recognizes and relates with his legitimate son at his level.

Apostle Paul says this in 1 Corinthians 13:11,

> "When I was a child, I spoke as a child, I understood as a child, I thought as a child; but when I became a man, I put away childish things."

This verse suggests to us the existence of different stages in a Christian's process. The father needs to act accordingly to properly support his son in his respective stage. I have had the blessing to see many of my spiritual sons pass from infancy to adolescence and from adolescence to spiritual adulthood. When they were infants, I treated them as infants. I expected them to make mistakes often. I expected certain spiritual lessons to be repeated many times to them before they were mastered. Patience toward my sons was very important to me in that stage. The relationship I had with them in that stage was that of a spiritual adult toward a spiritual child. When these babies grew in the faith to the state of spiritual adulthood, I changed my way of relating with them. Since they had grown in maturity and had foundation and greater depth in spiritual truths, I would still relate to them as sons, but sons that are no longer children but spiritual adults. They are adults that are capable of having autonomy with spiritual gifts that are not only identified, but understood and manifested in their ministries. They are ministers that are able to minister adequately; sons that do not only receive support but are also able to support the vision given by God to their spiritual authority. They are mature spiritual sons that are still teachable and yet used by God to counsel others in the ministry. The authentic spiritual father is able to make the transition from the relationship of father-infant to father-teenager to father-adult. This is so relevant since so many saints are choked in a rigid regime under a spiritual authority who has failed to recognize that they are no longer spiritual infants. Those who they see as children are really matured adults ready to receive spiritual responsibility commensurate to their spiritual growth. Therefore, the authentic spiritual father brings support that is adequate and conforms to the spiritual stage of his spiritual children's destiny.

Spiritual Security

The capacity to be used by God to bring spiritual security to his sons is another portion of the spiritual father's grace. There is a special anointing granted to the father for the spiritual security of his spiritual children. There is havoc that the devil cannot wreak on a saint that stays under authority of his spiritual father. The Bible says,

Exodus 32:30-33

"Now it came to pass on the next day that Moses said to the people, 'You have committed a great sin. So now I will go up to the Lord; perhaps I can make atonement for your sin.' Then Moses returned to the Lord and said, 'Oh, these people have committed a great sin, and have made for themselves a god of gold! Yet now, if You will forgive their sin but if not, I pray, blot me out of Your book which You have written.' And the Lord said to Moses, 'Whoever has sinned against Me, I will blot him out of My book.'"

Numbers 14:11-20

"Then the Lord said to Moses: 'How long will these people reject Me?...I will strike them with the pestilence and disinherit them' ...And Moses said to the Lord: "Then the Egyptians will hear it, for by Your might You brought these people up from among them, and they will tell it to the inhabitants of this land. They have heard that You, Lord, are among these people; that You, Lord, are seen face to face and Your cloud stands above them, and You go before

them in a pillar of cloud by day and in a pillar of fire by night. Now if You kill these people as one man, then the nations which have heard of Your fame will speak, saying, "Because the Lord was not able to bring this people to the land which He swore to give them, therefore He killed them in the wilderness" ...Pardon the iniquity of this people, I pray, according to the greatness of Your mercy, just as You have forgiven this people, from Egypt even until now.' Then the Lord said: 'I have pardoned, according to your word.'"

In these portions of Scripture, Moses intercedes for the people of Israel who had sinned against God. Because of his God-given mandate as the spiritual authority over the people of God, and according to his privileged relationship as spiritual guardian of the people of God, the Lord honoured his petition and forgave the sin of the people of Israel. The spiritual father has the capacity to intercede to the Father and have special attention from God with respect to the people he is called to nurture and protect.

In fact, the devil cannot do what he wants with a people under the spiritual covering of a servant that was mandated by God to lead that people. When a spiritual father raises his voice to God for his spiritual son, there is a special attention given by heaven. There is a level of attack of the Kingdom of darkness that cannot reach a people under spiritual authority.

10

Attitude of the Father his Son

The Word of God gives us several examples of the father-son relationship. This relationship is very special and is seen by certain traits. Observe a spiritual father who manifests an unconditional love for his son. He does not love him according to what he does, but for who he is to him. Your spiritual father should not love you according to the gifts that you have, but for the gift that you are. You do not have to perform to impress him because his only desire is to see you succeed in your destiny in Christ Jesus. He is willing and ready to do what is necessary for the fulfillment of this spiritual objective. Unfortunately, in this season in the Body of Christ we see many counterfeits take the title of father, but they only see in this self-proclamation a way to abuse a minister that is in search of the supervision and spiritual covering of a father. Notice the authentic father seeks not to receive, but to give. He gives of himself for the spiritual, physical, and material success of his spiritual son. Your problem is his problem, your pain is his pain, and your failure is his failure as much as your success is his success and your victory his victory. He is not intimidated by your gifting, your accomplishments and success. He is not jealous of what you have. The more you are thrust forth, the more he is blessed. Your blessings bring him joy and not sorrow. Your success gives him encouragement and not discouragement. He does not seek for his glory as your father, but your growth as a son. It will not be how he can benefit from you but how you can benefit from what he has. This is the heart of an authentic father for the relationship he has with his spiritual son.

11

Attitude of a Son Towards his Father

GENESIS 12:4

"So Abram departed as the Lord had spoken to him, and Lot went with him. And Abram was seventy-five years old when he departed from Haran."

GENESIS 17:15-16

"Then God said to Abraham, 'As for Sarai your wife, you shall not call her name Sarai, but Sarah shall be her name. And I will bless her and also give you a son by her; then I will bless her, and she shall be a mother of nations; kings of peoples shall be from her.'"

It is important to grasp the attitude of a son, for as much as it is relevant to recognize the characteristics of a spiritual father, it is also significant to recognize the proper attitude that a spiritual son should have. Notice that in a congregation many people come for many reasons. Not everyone that is under a man of God in a vision is a son. It goes without saying that there are people in the assemblies of saints that are not even children of God. In fact, when a minister is doing a serious spiritual work in a region, the Kingdom of darkness will send its agents to try to hinder the ministry and its fruit. Therefore, you should not be surprised to learn that witches, satanists, and occultists can be assigned to your assembly if it is really doing an effective spiritual work for our Lord Jesus. Nonetheless, in a congregation there are also Christians who are really saved and who participate in church for their spiritual growth. What a blessing it would be to have all the born again children of a church to be spiritual sons of that assembly. Albeit, often it is not so. The circumstances surrounding each believer's entrance into a particular church may vary. There are those born in the house and truly sons of that house, and others groomed in another house who end up in that house. Hence, in the latter group they are not sons of the new house but could still fulfill their destiny in that house. They might not be sons from the house but be a blessing in the fulfilling of the local vision and be blessed by the local house to accomplish their call without being a full-fledged son of that house. In other cases, some saints can be born in another house and realize that the spiritual leader of this new local house is truly his spiritual father, by reason of the fruit in his life and not only by title. There are some saints that may be sent by God to an assembly for a season before continuing their spiritual journey in some other mandated congregation. There are some others that may be sons of another minister, but because of circumstances beyond their control, they may end up being led by the Spirit of God to another congregation to complete their journey and reach their destiny. Therefore, even though it would be spiritually beneficial that all the saints in a congregation be spiritual sons to the spiritual father of the house, there are nonetheless, in the congregation, saints that are there for different reasons; they have different motives, having a different kind of relationship with the spiritual father in the house. I nevertheless want to touch some traits of a son to help you identify the sons in a spiritual house or at least help you know your status in your congregation concerning sonship.

A son in a local house stands out by the way he reacts to the vision of the assembly. The son will carry the vision of his father as his own. The vision of his father is his vision. He will not dissociate himself from the vision of his spiritual father. He will use the language of the family. He will speak of "us", and "our". He will want the best for the local family; he will want to see the advancement of the local vision while others in the family might simply want to benefit from the vision. These latter premeditatedly would be more comfortable using an individualistic language, speaking in the first person "I", "me", "my", and "mine". Therefore, what counts and has value to their eyes is "my problem, my need, my prayer, my situation"; the needs of the vision matter less. When such a saint needs ministry, the elders of the house need to be available immediately If they are not, they stigmatize the ministry as lacking love, accusing its ministers of having no time for them. Everything must be stopped for their needs to be met. The son who has the heart for the vision and the spiritual family can put his own needs aside for a while for the greater need of the vision. He will be more understanding if a delay is needed for his needs to be met. On the other hand, he that is there for his own ends might even leave the church because he did not have his wishes met.

The son will do everything for the edification and protection of the vision, since he considers the vision of his spiritual father as his own. Opposition that comes to the ministry will not be an occasion for him to leave, neither to blame or doubt the vision. He will not participate in backbiting or negative criticism thrown by the devil and the flesh against the vision. Although he wants to stand for the truth, he will not use this prerogative as an instrument to criticize and destroy the vision that has built and blessed him. Note that there is a difference between being a carnal fanatic that is spiritually hoodwinked in a vision and being a son. The son is not blind to the weaknesses or what is problematic in the vision of his spiritual father, but he will do all that is within his power to be an instrument to improve it.

There are carnal Christians whose pleasure is to bring up the past whereas the spiritual son does not recall what has been dealt with. He would rather go forward with the past experience that has brought maturity through the adversity.

The attitude of the son toward the people in the congregation will be different to that of the saints that are simply participants in the services. The son will work for the well-being of the people. He will take pleasure in connecting the newcomer to the vision and to the spiritual family. He will not try to attract the ones he shares with to himself, but instead introduce them to the spiritual father and to the corporate spiritual vision of the house. When a son has something go wrong, he will think no evil, but he will rather share the thoughts and profound feelings of his heart with the appropriate minister in order to not give access to the enemy or the flesh to turn him away from God's divine plan. His reaction to a problematic situation will be conciliatory. Even though he would need to be corrected, that is for him a blessing. In fact, the son stands out in the way he reacts to corrections. He accepts the sayings of Ecclesiastes 7:5 that declares, "It is better to hear the rebuke of the wise than for a man to hear the song of fools." The son submits himself to the authority of the spiritual father and recognizes his divine role to correct him and to give him the necessary perfecting to reach his destiny. Some saints however wrestle with the idea of being under authority and will seek constantly to redefine authority and the leaders' role in their lives.

A son will take great pleasure in honouring his spiritual father. He does not have to be forced to seize the opportunity when it presents itself to give honour to whom honour is due. Truly, he will not be part of the congregation that minimizes or despises the honour that is due to the spiritual father. He recognizes that one should not only speak of honour, respect or reverence, but also demonstrate them. It is not enough to only meditate on it and believe it, for a declaration without any action is only a pretension. Many unfortunately believe that it is exaggerated for a Christian to show a marked reverence and honour to his spiritual father. This line of thought is very often the lethal influence of the spirit of insubmission and disrespect that affects many regions of the world. In North America, these spirits are rampant. They possess many saints. They refute any form of respect, honour or other principle that concerns spiritual authority and the way they should properly conduct themselves toward them. They soulishly convince themselves that proper reverence and respect to spiritual authority is fleshly worship of men or evidence of a subtle power of spiritual abuse. Please know that a distinguished respect for spiritual authority is a biblical principle that is seen in different ways.

Respect manifested by acknowledgement

2 SAMUEL 12:26-28

"Now Joab fought against Rabbah of the people of Ammon, and took the royal city. And Joab sent messengers to David, and said, 'I have fought against Rabbah, and I have taken the city's water supply. Now therefore, gather the rest of the people together and encamp against the city and take it, lest I take the city and it be called after my name.'"

2 SAMUEL 18:1-3

"And David numbered the people who were with him, and set captains of thousands and captains of hundreds over them... And the king said to the people, 'I also will surely go out with you myself.' But the people answered, 'You shall not go out! For if we flee away, they will not care about us; nor if half of us die, will they care about us? But you are worth ten thousand of us now. For you are now more help to us in the city.'"

We see in these two portions of Scripture the respect of spiritual authority manifested by the acknowledgement of the person bearing that authority. The mighty men of valour of David and the people of God acknowledged who David was to them. They understood his role and great value as their leader. Joab, the captain of the host, strictly refused to officially enter the city that was besieged, not wanting to receive a glory that was not his, as captain of the army, but was the portion of the king of the Kingdom. And the people understood that if they had to lose someone in war, their leader was worth at least ten thousand men, a figurative way of saying that he was of great importance to them. In fact, they understood that they could lose a great deal of men but could not afford to lose their leader in war. They therefore sought to give him special protection, acknowledging how important he was in their eyes.

Respect Manifested by the Naming

2 KINGS 2:12
"And Elisha saw it, and he cried out, 'My father, my father, the chariot of Israel and its horsemen!'"

JOHN 1:38
"Then Jesus turned, and seeing them following, said to them, 'What do you seek?' They said to him, 'Rabbi' (which is to say, when translated, Teacher), 'Where are you staying?"

Respect of spiritual authority is also manifested in the title or naming of such a person. Elisha had a biological father, yet he manifested his respect for his spiritual father Elijah by affectionately calling out to him "My father, my father". The disciples of the Lord, in the time when they had him in their midst, called him "Rabbi". In this 21st century in many nations, but predominantly in the western world, we are witnessing the tangible manifestation of disrespect in our societies.

Unfortunately, this trend is also visible in the Body of Christ. Many Christians, in their ignorance, and also out of rebellion, refuse to show any type of distinguished respect whatsoever to a spiritual authority. Instead, they simply want to stand on their spiritually corrupt belief that all Christians are the same and should be treated equally even with regards to respect. Truly, all Christians are equally loved in the sight of God, but this does not however discard the principle of respect to spiritual fathers and delegated authorities that carry the authority of God. Therefore, there are some spiritual positions and functions that require special respect and honour from the rest of the saints.

The Bible is clear concerning this fact:

HEBREWS 13:17

"Obey those who rule over you, and be submissive, for they watch out for your souls, as those who must give account. Let them do so with joy and not with grief, for that would be unprofitable for you."

1 TIMOTHY 5:17

"Let the elders who rule well be counted worthy of double honour, especially those who labour in the word and doctrine."

It is therefore biblical to show respect and honour to a person in authority over the children of God. Apostle Paul speaking to the people of Thessalonica declares to them in 1 Thessalonians 5:12,

"Now also we beseech you, brethren, get to know those who labour among you (Recognize them for what they are, acknowledge and appreciate and respect them all) – your leaders who are over you in the Lord and those who warn and kindly reprove and exhort you."

Therefore, it is the will of God for the saints to recognize the spiritual leaders that are over them and show them special consideration and noted respect. Notice that Apostle Paul does not admonish the saints to have a hidden and subtle affection for them, but he insists that they recognize them for what they are, acknowledge, appreciate and respect them openly. It is also very clear why this must be done: It is because of their ministry to the saints. The quality of their ministry and who they are to the Body of Christ qualify them to receive such respect and the special consideration of the saints under their spiritual covering. The spiritual father and the elders in a congregation are called to take care of the flock that is under their charge.

ACTS 20:28
"Therefore take heed to yourselves and to all the flock, among which the Holy Spirit has made you overseers, to shepherd the church of God which He purchased with His own blood."

A spiritual father and the elders have been established over a particular group of saints called a local church. They have the responsibility of overseeing, covering spiritually by prayer, protecting and securing against all attacks of the enemy (that are against the flock and the Word), training and teaching. The spiritual father is the spiritual authority over the saints that are under his covering, and of the college of elders. Understand that this is not control but a biblical reality. The Church needs to grasp this truth if it wants to stand out in this contemporary society that is anti-respect, and that operates with hardly any accountability or affiliation to any ministry. Many do not want to be accountable to anyone in this generation. They want to live without any authority, yet they still want to be in an assembly and benefit from all its riches. However, you shall know the truth and the truth shall set you free.

Reverence and honour toward a spiritual head are principles that are seen throughout the Word of God. Saul inquired for the counsels of Prophet Samuel, but would not accept to go without bringing a present to the man of God to honour him. Now, for the ones that are bound by the disrespect of our modern day society, this protocol might seem very far-fetched, totally absurd and heretical.

1 SAMUEL 9:6-8

"And he said to him, 'Look now there is in this city a man of God, and he is an honourable man; all that he says surely comes to pass. So let us go there; perhaps he can show us the way that we should go.' Then Saul said to his servant, 'But look, if we go, what shall we bring the man? For the bread in our vessels is all gone, and there is no present to bring to the man of God. What do we have?' And the servant answered Saul again and said, 'Look, I have here at hand one-fourth of a shekel of silver. I will give that to the man of God, to tell us our way.'"

Therefore, Saul understood the respect and honour due to the man of God and henceforth inherited the favour of God. In the same episode, it is told that the people of God would not eat until Prophet Samuel blessed their food. Does that seem exaggerated to you? Not at all, this is simply respect and honour to the spiritual father of the nation of God in that time.

1 SAMUEL 9:11-13

"As they went up the hill to the city, they met some young women going out to draw water, and said to them, 'Is the seer here?' And they answered them and said, 'Yes, there he is, just ahead of you. Hurry now; for today he came to this city, because there is a sacrifice of the people on the high place. As soon as you come into the city, you will surely find him before he goes up to the high place to eat. For the people will not eat until he comes, because he must bless the sacrifice; afterward those who are invited will eat. Now therefore, go up, for about this time you will find him."

Now when the Lord revealed to Prophet Samuel that the young Saul was promoted to be the next king of His people, the prophet offered him a service worthy of a future king.

The Bible tells us in 1 Samuel 9:22-24,

"Now Samuel took Saul and his servant and brought them into the hall, and had them sit in the place of honour among those who were invited; there were about thirty persons. And Samuel said to the cook, 'Bring the portion which I

gave you, of which I said to you, "Set it apart"." So the cook
took up the thigh with its upper part and set it before Saul..."

Prophet Samuel had asked his cook to serve the thigh with its upper part to Saul, because according to the law of Moses that part was given to dignitaries.

LEVITICUS 7:32-35
"Also the right thigh you shall give to the priest as a heave
offering from the sacrifices of your peace offerings...This is
the consecrated portion for Aaron and his sons..."

My question for you is the following: Would you have done or even thought of honouring your spiritual father or even a servant of God in that fashion or do you believe that this is idolatry and blasphemous against God to show such reverence toward a man?

Respect and honour to a man of God should also be extended to protocol in having an audience with him. Notice, this does not mean that he should not be accessible, but giving due consideration to his "space" and how he is approached is a mark of respect.

The Bible says in John 12:20-22,

"Now there were certain Greeks among those who came up
to worship at the feast. Then they came to Philip, who was
from Bethsaida of Galilee, and asked him, saying, 'Sir, we
wish to see Jesus.' Philip came and told Andrew, and in turn
Andrew and Philip told Jesus."

We see in this portion of Scripture some Greeks that wanted to see Jesus. Although Jesus was accessible enough to eat privately with Zacchaeus at his house, there was nevertheless a certain protocol to approach the man of God. I truly believe that this was for reverence and protection, for surely not all those who followed Jesus greatly appreciated him, although He was a blessing for the nation. There was therefore a precaution taken for those who wanted to approach Jesus, which was probably also to allow a certain level of privacy to the man of God. Today, when a protocol is established to approach a man of God, the ignorant cry out that it is heresy, idolatry, the worshipping of a man. What ignorance!

The Bible again tells us in Acts 5:12-13,

> *"And through the hands of the apostles many signs and wonders were done among the people. And they were all with one accord in Solomon's Porch. Yet none of the rest dared join them, but the people esteemed them highly."*

In this chapter, the disciples of Jesus grew in maturity and became the apostles of Jerusalem's first century church doing the work of bishops, or spiritual leadership, of the church. After the clear demonstration of the power of God through them with the miracle of judgement of Ananias and Sapphira, the Bible says that great fear came upon all the church and upon all who heard these things. This great reverence, which came as a result of the manifestation of the power of God through the apostles, led to an added outbreak of miracles, signs, wonders, and a great harvest of souls. The latter outbreak also provoked a particular respect and honour of the men of God in the church of Jerusalem. The Bible tells us that none of the rest of the people of God in Jerusalem dared join the apostles, but the people esteemed them highly. In our modern day society, for the person who is ignorant to the principle of respect and honour to authority, this would truly be considered man-worship and unclean adulation. Maybe some would even say that it is demonically led, thinking that it might have been the men of God who bound the people. On the contrary, the respect and honour exhibited towards the company of apostles in Acts 5 is simply an acknowledgement of the anointing that is on the leaders, and the consecration that needs to be protected to help them to be even more effective in their divine mandate. Human nature normally likes getting used to someone and likes rendering all things common.

Proverbs 25:17 tells us to

"*Seldom set foot in your neighbour's house, lest he become weary of you and hate you.*"

In other words, habits can become sin. This is also a reality in ministry. The habit of having too much proximity with the man of God can become sin for he that does not have that particular call from God.

Unnecessary proximity can result in disrespect and lack of reverence from the saint that is not properly groom for that. The anointed of God carries a special anointing to lead and take care of the children of God. If the people of God get too comfortable with him, they will contaminate and short-circuit the efficacy of this anointing to bless them. This in return would bring negative repercussions on the people of God, because God respects and honours the anointing and the authority that He has placed on his leaders. Romans 13:2 says that if someone resists authority he certainly brings judgement on himself. Many Christians are actually living hardships in their lives due to judgement they brought on themselves by resisting authority. Therefore, bad attitude and action toward leaders, and, for that matter, their spiritual father who is called to take care of their spiritual growth, will surely lead to judgement upon one's life. There will be a blessing attached to your proper attitude and action toward your spiritual father.

The Bible tells us in Matthew 10:41,

"He who receives a prophet in the name of a prophet shall receive a prophet's reward..."

The text assumes that it is possible to receive a man of God, but not in the quality or appropriate protocol that goes with his calling. It is not sufficient therefore to merely honour and respect one's spiritual father or other dignitaries of the Lord, but it must be done in a manner befitting their calling. It is not enough just to honour and respect one's spiritual father, but it needs to be done with the quality of who he is in one's life.

Conclusion

Our God, who provides for the needs of nations, is answering their cry and special paternal need in this season. He is raising up spiritual fathers who will be fathers not only in word and for selfish purposes, but in action and in truth. We will recognize them not by their words, but by their hearts and their abundant fruits, the fruits of restoration in this generation suffering from a lack of paternal presence. The nation once was fatherless, but God is raising up fathers that are identified, trained, mandated and sent to restore a necessary element to the blossoming of a strong society. The presence and ministry of spiritual fathers are able to raise up strong saints. Henceforth these saints will be able to penetrate and positively affect the different societal systems.

Equipped to preach and teach as much as exemplifying the role of the father in the family cell, the spiritual father will answer the need to restore families which are the essential foundation of a healthy society. The fatherless nations have been crying out, the Lord Jesus Christ has answered. Spiritual fathers are released to transition the church into its destiny and accomplish the mandate of expanding the Kingdom of God on the earth to the glory of the Father.